Martin the Guitar
in the BIG CITY

by HARRY MUSSELWHITE
Illustrated by **BRIAN BARR**

From Harry:
"Martin the Guitar in the Big City" goes out to all the wonderful musicians who have contributed their art, wisdom, and talent to my career over the years. Thanks, as always go to my family and my terrific publisher, Ron Middlebrook.

From Brian:
To my wife, Carrie, my mom, Angie, and my sister, Brianne. Thank you for always encouraging me and never being embarrassed about talking me up to strangers, even when I ask you not to do that.

Words and Story ©2018 by Harry Musselwhite

Illustrations ©2018 by Brian Barr

Art Direction and Design by Monica Sheppard

Visit **www.martintheguitar.com** for access to the great soundtrack for the "Martin" Books and don't forget to like us and follow our news on FaceBook and Twitter!

ISBN: 978-1-57424-362-8

Copyright © 2018 Centerstream Publishing, LLC
P.O. Box 17878 –Anaheim Hills, CA 92817

www.centerstream-usa.com

All rights reserved. All rights for publication and distribution are reserved.

No part of this book may be reproduced in any form or by any electronic or mechanical means including information storage and retrieval systems without permission in writing from the publisher, except by reviewers who may quote brief passages in review. This book is in no way intended to infringe on the intellectual property rights of any party. All products, brands, and names represented are trademarks or registered trademarks of their respective companies; information in this book was derived from the author's independent research and was not authorized, furnished, or approved by other parties.

The C.F. Martin & Company, 510 Sycamore Street, Nazareth, Pennsylvania, has granted "Martin the Guitar in the Big City" a non-exclusive license in the preparation, printing, reprinting, publication, republication, marketing, distribution, and sale of the Book, and any advertising or promotional materials directly relating to and mentioning the book.

Martin the Guitar and his owner, the famous folksinger Robert, finished their last song. Robert bowed and held Martin proudly for all to see. The audience cheered.

Martin and Robert stayed backstage and listened as their friends Dorothy and Laura sang. The two women, who called themselves "The Violets", were wonderful singers. Robert smiled as the two blended their voices in sweet harmony.

Martin and Robert cheered as they ended their last song. The crowd roared as Dorothy and Laura took a bow. They waved to the happy audience as they left the stage.

Martin was so proud because Laura was playing his friend Morgan the Guitar. As she passed him, Morgan gave Martin a friendly wink. The next guitar to pass was Morgan's father, Archie the Archtop Guitar. When he looked at Martin he gave him a scowl.

Martin's smile changed to a frown.

Robert and "The Violets" went out to see their fans and sign autographs. All the excited instruments gathered in a room near the stage.

Martin stood next to Morgan.

"You were wonderful today," beamed Martin.

Morgan blushed.

"Thank you, Martin. You sounded terrific, too!" said Morgan.

A loud voice boomed from the other side of the room.

"Morgan, come over here and check your strings," commanded Archie.

"Coming, Daddy," said Morgan.

Martin looked down. He didn't think Archie liked him very much.

"Your father doesn't like me," whispered Martin.

"Give him a chance, he'll warm up to you," answered Morgan softly.

"Morgan!" shouted Archie.

"Coming," Morgan cheerfully answered.

Morgan and Archie talked quietly for a few moments and then Morgan called out, "Martin, my dad wants to speak with you."

Martin swallowed hard. He so wanted Archie to like him. Morgan was his newest friend, and he loved talking to her and sharing music.

Martin lifted up his head and walked proudly over to Archie.

"Yes sir?" he asked, his voice cracking with nerves.

Archie looked Martin over. Martin looked at the floor.

"Look at me, young guitar, when I talk with you!"

Martin looked up at Archie and tried to act bravely.

"Martin, I don't know if you have heard, but you and Robert have been invited to perform in the big hall in New York City. This is a huge honor. The concert hall is the most famous place to play music in the whole world."

Martin smiled from top to bottom.

"New York City!" he exclaimed, "Why that's where I'm from. I grew up in Mr. Beninato's music store."

"Hmmm," groaned Archie, "I suppose you used to live with all those brand new shiny instruments."

"Well, not all of them are new. Why, I have a friend name Strada who is very old, and she's one of the most famous violins in the world."

"Enough of those silly stories," snapped Archie. "You'd better get ready for the biggest night of your life, young man."

"Yes, sir, Mr. Archie," said Martin.

"And about my daughter, Morgan," said Archie, "perhaps you should spend more time with your music than her."

Martin stepped up.

"But Mr. Archie, she's my...."stammered Martin.

"Father!" shouted Morgan.

Archie and Martin turned toward an angry Morgan.

"I happen to like Martin very much, and if I want to talk to him, I will," said Morgan.

Morgan turned to her instrument case. Martin looked up at Archie.

"I promise I will do my best in New York City, Mr. Archie," said Martin.

Martin went over to his corner of the room. He looked down and he could hardly hide the big smile on his face.

"She said she liked me," whispered Martin.

On the day of the concert in New York City, all the musicians and instruments gathered at the famous hall to practice. They entered the building and looked at the pictures of all the famous musicians lining the hallways. This was a special place.

The musicians walked out on to the stage and prepared to play.

Robert and Martin the Guitar were the first to practice. In the middle of the first song, Martin really felt the music down deep. He was so proud to be in this musical place where so many of his musical heroes had made great music.

Suddenly something most terrible happened.

Martin broke a string.

Robert quickly took Martin backstage to change the string. Martin was upset, and he tried not to show Robert.

Robert looked down.

"Don't worry, Martin, these things happen. We'll be fine tonight. We'll make great music together," soothed Robert.

Quickly Martin had a new string and was back in tune.

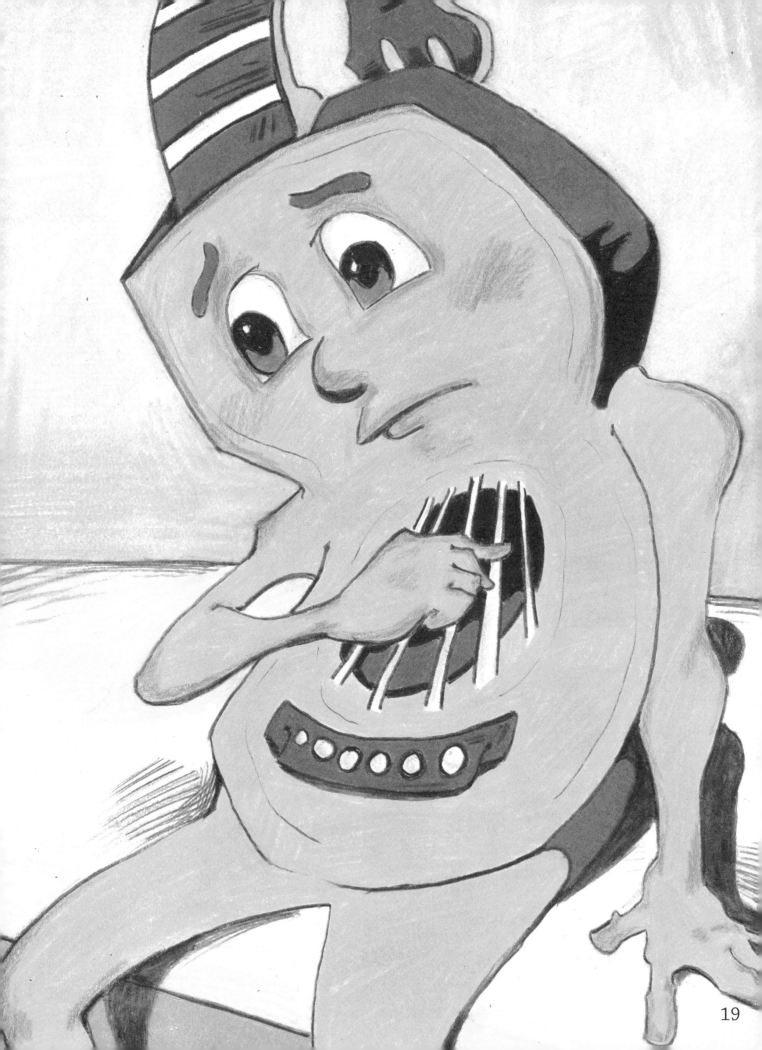

Archie waited for Martin at the rear of the stage.

"Well, well, you broke a string on the most famous stage in the world," snarled Archie.

Morgan stepped up.

"Daddy, you know well that you've broken strings before, and in some very important places," snapped Morgan.

Martin looked down and didn't say a word.

"Don't worry Martin, you are going to be wonderful tonight," said Morgan.

Martin smiled.

The audience filled the auditorium. Robert and Martin rejoiced as Robert's voice grew stronger with each new song. After each song, the audience clapped even louder.

Robert was so excited. He began to strum Martin's strings harder and harder. Robert grinned from ear to ear.

'Oh, oh, I'm going to break a string for sure," whispered Martin. Martin became very nervous.

Robert finished his song and spoke into the microphone.

"Folks, let us welcome some old friends of ours from Mr. Beninato's Music Shop, right here in New York City," said Robert.

The crowd cheered as Mr. Beninato walked out carrying none other than Strada the Violin. Behind her were Martin's friends Big D the Guitar, and Loar the Mandolin.

Martin was so happy to see his old friends.

As Strada passed Martin, she looked down and smiled.

"Don't forget what I taught you, young Martin, believe in yourself!" she whispered.

Martin took a deep breath as Robert counted off the song.

Martin's strings rang like church bells and all the other instruments played with full hearts. The crowd cheered and cheered.

After the concert, Morgan found Martin.

"Morgan, I didn't break a string! Not one!" exclaimed Martin.

"Martin, you were perfect. I don't think you've ever sounded better," cooed Morgan.

Morgan leaned over and kissed Martin.

Martin beamed with joy.

"You did it," boomed a big voice.

Archie stepped in front of Martin and Morgan.

"You showed greatness tonight, greatness," he proclaimed.

Archie turned to leave, but he stopped and turned around to face Martin.

"I'm proud of you," he smiled.

"We are ALL proud of you!" shouted Strada.

All the instruments burst into applause as Martin smiled at Morgan.

"This is the best night of my life," shouted Martin.

The End

Check out these great Martin books!

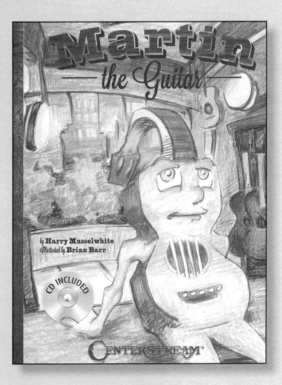

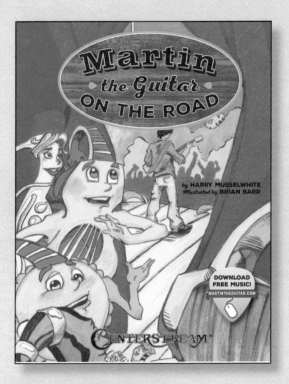

MARTIN THE GUITAR
by Harry Musselwhite
00001601 Book/CD Pack.....................$19.99

**MARTIN THE GUITAR
ON THE ROAD**
by Harry Musselwhite Illus. Brian Barr
00234198 Book/Online Audio...............$9.99

P.O. Box 17878 - Anaheim Hills, CA 92817
(714) 779-9390   www.centerstream-usa.com